Introduction

Table of Contents

1. A History of Debt
2. Debt is not bad
3. Head in the sand
4. Your Budget
5. Take Control
6. Reducing fixed and variable costs
7. Prioritise
8. Be Realistic
9. Set Goals
10. Understanding APR
11. Income Streams
12. Savings, Pensions and Compounding
13. Using Apps to Help
14. How to Remain Debt Free (Money Can't buy you happiness but!)
15. Spreadsheets to Help
16. Reference Material
17. Reminders
18. Materials

**Introduction,**

Thanks for buying this book I hope you find the information useful and easy to use, Please note this is not a get rich quick scheme type of book that promises ways to get out of debt quickly, However this book will help you get an overview and grip on your finances and within 3-6 months if you follow the suggestions in this book you should be able to feel less pressure over your finances and more in control.

Now you will have to make sacrifices along the way but at the same time this is not a book that tells you to live in a cave and eat baked beans for the rest of your life!

A little about myself, like you I got into debt which started when I was young and naive with my very first credit card, at this stage no one had taught me about financial planning or money management. I got into debt quite quickly, took out a loan and repeated the same mistakes. Then probably like you I needed a new loan to get a car so bought that used the credit card as I was overspending and relationship breakdowns did not help.

Over a period of time I amassed serious debts on credit cards as well as loans, So I took out more loans to pay of the credit cards and consolidate the debt, then more debt on the credit cards, then relationship breakdowns finding somewhere to live. If this sounds familiar then read on.

I am not going to on a tirade against how unfair this is etc.... This was all my doing I cannot blame anyone else, these were the choices I chose due to circumstances at the time.

Unfortunately, the education system does not teach you about basic budgeting and this can cause issues with debt and understanding debt but also with your future wealth management.

Having read many books on the subject of debt and psychology I put together my own plan to get me out of debt. Having followed this formula, I happy to say I am mostly debt free with a small amount on a credit card at an acceptable level and if you follow my ideas then you will be debt free within 24 months or at least have it down to a small amount.

Most books out there will just focus on your finances and forget about the most important thing, and that is your emotions and brain. In this book I hope to help you understand and realise that it is in your control and you do not have to live like a hermit to solve the issue (Let's face it you are already in most cases living month to month anyway!)

This is not be a book that assumes you have a great credit score and you can just go out and consolidate all your debt and everything will be rosy. We have tried that before and where did we end up?

I hope you enjoy this book I have tried to make it non-judgemental and hopefully it will help you understand yourself and how you can resolve your money issues.

I hope you will be surprised and happy with some of the suggestions I have written down.

Please also remember that any materials you require to help you along your way from this book will be freely available to you. (unlike some books I have read where you have to pay to get additional content or they try and sell you additional materials) all you will need to do is email me at debtbudgetandcompunding@gmail.com with your request in the subject and I will respond. And remember if this book has helped you then feel free to drop me a line with any comments and suggestions or better yet leave a review!

Remember that if you are in serious financial difficulty, I do suggest you speak to one of the many charities out there who will be able to help and offer advice. Do not be afraid to talk to someone about this, it may be in certain cases that they will be able to speak to lenders on your behalf if you are not comfortable with talking to them. Or drop me an email and I will try to point you in the right direction, after all I have been where you are so I know how you are feeling and will happily give advice where I can.

**1, History of Debt**


Personal loans in one form or another have been around since the Greeks and Romans where a lender would set up a stall and offer loans to qualified customers. We have many historical records of people and institutions loaning people monies, whether it be because of a bad harvest or to buy an animal for the farm. Debt was always carefully managed with the exception of a few unscrupulous lenders whom lent to people who did not have the collateral to borrow from established peoples.

Personal card debt is a fairly new concept which has only been with us as we know it for the last 50 years. It was the invention of the first credit card in the 1950's that helped it take off. Originally, they were advertised as a time saving device rather than a form of credit, and it was not until the 1970's that the credit card really took off with the advertisements in magazines. With this also came the adverts for time saving devices in the kitchen and store credit and then in the 1980's we had the rental era and Hire Purchase (HP) as well as personal loans. We now as a nation (UK) spend on average £15 Billion pounds a month on credit cards!

Credit card debt has been growing steadily since the 1990's, With the UK, USA and Australia as the most intensive credit card users

In the UK the average consumer in has 2.4 credit cards. We now spend on average £15 Billion pounds a month on credit cards! This is five times more than we were spending in 1993!.

The current personal debt (Excluding Mortgages) in the UK is at £200 Billion pounds, the average person owes on average £8,000. (£15,000 if you include student debt) this does not include mortgage payments either. On Average 25% of these consumers are struggling to make ends meet, with an additional 10% of these consumers already maxing out credit cards to live.

What have banks been doing to help consumers with this issue I hear you ask? Lend you more money!

I am afraid if you are looking at the banks for a solution you will only find more loans coming your way!

The only way to take charge of the financial situation you are in is by you looking at it in its entirety. After all banks are businesses who report to shareholders and how does a bank make money? by selling loans. You only have to look at the way that mortgages were handed out in America and the UK, or the PPI scandal in the UK to see that they will try and get money out of you anyway they can!

We will not look at bank's morality and ethics in this book as there has been plenty written and spoken about on this subject, after all this book is about you and helping you!

## 2, Debt is not Bad

The first thing we need to know is debt is not bad! Having debt is ok as long as you can manage it without financially struggling,

For example, I know of one person whom has a car on a Personal Contract Plan (PCP) this is whereby they are renting the vehicle for a fixed term (usually between 12-36 Months) and hand it back at the end of the contract. Think of it as renting a car from a rental company but not for a week but for 1-3 years, it sounds better in months though doesn't it as months not years (more on this later)

This means they can have a new car with no worries of breakdown and maintenance for the duration of the rental. Now they looked at the pros and cons and decided in their situation this worked for them, (If you are interested, they got a Skoda Octavia for £169.00 per month) this means that they pay £4,550 over the term of the rental. So rather than outlaying £5000 on a used car they have a brand-new vehicle for two years, however at the end of the rental period they have to return it.

Now the above scenario is not for everybody as they have to find that money each month to pay for the motor vehicle.

Credit Cards

Credit cards are useful to give yourself piece of mind on large purchases, as long as the value of goods is between a certain amount you can put any amount on your credit card and you will in most cases be covered in law by most countries via there chargeback scheme.

This means should the goods not arrive, go faulty (Dependant on time) and you get no joy or response from the seller, you can apply for a refund via your card company.

There are several caveats on this some do not cover 3rd part payment systems (Apple Pay, PayPal etc..) and some do not cover purchases made on prototype stage projects (Kickstarter and Indiegogo for example)

Just remember to pay the spend off each month!!

Loans, sometimes a loan is necessary dependant on its use, People use loans all the time mainly as mortgages. Buying a business or an outlay on capital equipment (with the exception of the first one, unless you are looking at buying a second property for an income stream more on this in chapter 10)

But the one thing they all have in common is they are not using the loan to consolidate debt, they are using it to help them create wealth long term, this is what you need to understand moving forward, it is ok to use your cards and take loans and be in debt as long as the reason you did it is to help create wealth for you and your family long term.

## 3, Head in the sand

I have been there and done that, A letter from the bank comes through the door and I do not open it as I know what it will say, as if leaving it a few days will magickly change the contents!

An unarranged overdraft or late payment fee, no payment received this month, need to pay double next month and before you know it you are paying out more in fees than you could afford, payday comes and you pay the minimum to keep the wolf from the door, until the next month when it all starts again so the vicious cycle continues.

Now we need to get out of this mindset, we cannot focus on being the victim with a poverty mindset, we need to remember Life happens for you, not to you!!

The reason you are in this situation in the main will be choices you have made in the past (This does not apply to all people as I realise things are getting more expensive) but my point is you have the ability to change it!!

Some of the issues may come down to lack of experience, confidence and poor management, remember though this book will help you to focus on helping yourself!

What I suggest you do is sit down whenever you are relaxed and can concentrate and look through your accounts to work out exactly how much money you owe and to whom. At this point do not worry about APR (we will cover that later in chapter 9). What we need to know is exactly how much debt we owe right now. The great thing about the internet is this information is all at our fingertips.

So, the first thing I would recommend is going and registering with a credit checker. Experian and Equifax used to be the two main ones offering this service with a free trial then chargeable, however you can now use the likes of Noodle and clear score amongst others, Bear in mind they are generally about 4 weeks behind the credit on your card and the amount owed on your loan. But at least this will give you an idea of how much debt you have accrued.

Now put the total on a piece of paper split in two (loans and credit cards, as we are concentrating on the latter to begin with) or post it note and a realistic date of when you would like to be debt free. Don't worry about the size of the number just put it somewhere you can see it as a daily reminder, the quicker you tackle a problem head on the easier it is to deal with (I will cover this in chapter 8)

Now we have our total debt we can break down how much is owed to who, I suggest a spreadsheet so it will look something like this.

| Credit Cards | Balance | Credit Limit | Min Payment | APR |
|---|---|---|---|---|
| Bank 1 Credit Card | £2,300 | £2,500 | £40 | 20% |
| Bank 2 Credit Card | £2,410 | £2,500 | £60 | 30% |
| Bank 3 Credit Card | £800 | £1,000 | £15 | 20% |

| Loans | Balance | Repayment | Date finishes |
|---|---|---|---|
| Loan 1 Remaining | £4,890 | £100 | 49 Months |
| (£6000 Loan over 60 Months £100 per month repayment) | | | |
| Loan 2 Remaining | £1,800 | £105 | 18 Months |
| (£5000 Loan over 48 Months, £105 per month repayment) | | | |
| Overdraft | £500 | £15 | |

So what we have above is our balance on the credit card with minimum payment and APR, then our amount outstanding on loans (I class them as fixed costs, but more on this later) We then put the date the loan finishes so you have an idea on when those funds will be free (We will look at this in chapter 8) and our overdraft, With the monthly fees this incurs.

Now congratulations you have done the hard part and are now either surprised or extremely scared! Don't worry about the number at the moment, now go off have a cup of tea or something stronger as a reward, because believe it or not this is probably the hardest bit you have done.

So, in this example we have a credit facility of £6,000 but we are currently using £5,510 of this (92%) Most banks like your debt on cards to be around 60%, this is when you will start seeing your credit score increase rapidly and this will be one of our first goals (See chapter 8), We then have £6,690 in personal loans and a £500 overdraft. So, in total we have £12,700 of personal debt.

Now I am assuming you cannot get a personal loan to consolidate all your debt or even just your credit card debt. So, what can we do?

## 4, Your Budget

The average family in the UK overspends by approximately 10% each month of their salary, which means more pressure being put on credit cards and then guess what we are back in the vicious cycle of debt and loans and struggling to get by.

So how can we beat this, the first thing to do is start a budget (there are plenty of books and references on this available, but I find a lot of them over complicated)

I suggest using a spreadsheet to use as a simple budget to get you started.

I have one you can use if you email me at debtbudgetandcompunding@gmail.com and put budget in the title

Always round up to the nearest Pound/Dollar or whichever currency you are using.


Example


The below is based on a family with one child, one parent earning the UK average wage and one parent in part time work, with the UK average Mortgage.

| | |
|---|---|
| Income Streams | £2400 |
| Fixed Costs | £1065 |
| Loans | £220 (We will include overdraft charges in this) |
| Total Fixed Costs | £1285 (Fixed costs plus Loans) |
| Credit Cards | £115 (Worked on Minimum payments) |
| Sub Total | £1100 (Fixed Costs plus Credit Cards minus Income) |
| Variable Expenses | £1000 (Food, Car, Entertainment, Clothing Etc…) |
| Total Free Money | £100 (Sub Total minus Variable Expenses) |

To find your direct debits and standing orders check you bank statements.

If you date them it will help and again round up to the nearest 0, In most cases your outgoing fixed costs will generally come out of your account after payday. But some will be later and we need to list these to ensure we know where our income is going.

So, as you can see on the above this family would have £100 left to use that is before unknown costs then come in.

So now we know where our finances are how do we get out of this cycle and reduce our expenses/debt?

Congratulations on making it this far let me tell you, you should now be feeling more like a lion than the ostrich ready to tackle your debt and move your goal towards financial freedom.

## 5 Taking Control

Please remember if you have done step 2 and you find your finances are in a really bad situation then you need help. Again, remember There is no shame in admitting that things have spiralled out of control, I would strongly suggest talking to one of the many charities that can help with personal debt finance,

You will not be the first person to have rung them and it is better to talk to your creditors earlier rather than later. If you need help or guidance with this email me at debtbudgetandcompunding@gmail.com and I will send some contacts for you to call. I will also list some of them at the back of this book

There are things we can do though to take back control and I suggest taking the next few steps

If you are a couple open a joint bank account and move all of your fixed costs (Direct Debits, Standing Orders, etc...) to this account and each person put a set amount in each month to cover food and direct debits. This will ensure they are paid and you know how much you have left for other items.

If you are single then I would still suggest doing this as you will be placing a barrier between your costs and spending money.

Then I would also look at opening a savings account with any bank, whichever you feel comfortable using. But make sure you can access the funds quickly and easily

The reason we are looking at a separate account for our fixed costs is that as humans we are good at responding to visual stimulants. By removing our fixed costs, we can see then see what we are left with as our amount to live on for the next month.

Also, by opening a savings account then again you are sending a positive to our brain that we are going to squirrel a little bit of cash away each month.

Remember there are also a plethora of apps available to help you control your budgeting and spending (see chapter 12)

Credit cards

In an ideal world I would suggest paying of 10% of each credit card minimum per month, but as you can see this couple are not in a position to do this.

So what can we do?

Firstly I would suggest speaking to your providers to see if they can put you on to a different credit card with a lower APR to help ease the minimum payments (keep the payments the same if you can as this will help with the interest that is being accrued, If your card is with your current bank I suggest booking a financial meeting with them to open the joint account and then ask this when you are there)

Now what I will say next will go against everything you will have been told by everyone who has ever written a book on the subject of financial planning.

It is to look at overpaying the card with the smallest balance on it first. There shocked you didn't I!

The conflict with this information from most financial people will be that you either pay off the largest bill first, or pay off the highest APR first, whilst both of these positions come from sound accounting practices, they seem to forget one big thing in play. Your brain and more importantly your emotions!

Whilst your brain is an incredible machine it Is also very fragile especially with the Fight or flight syndrome (I recommend a very good book on this subject, the Chimp Paradox by Dr Steve Peters who explains this better than I ever could, also it is a book that helps you understand stress and emotions)

If you have a large amount of debt on one credit card you will look at the payments you are making and see that the number is not really moving so will be less motivated to carry on after a short amount of time. (Ask me how I know this!?)

Let me show you why.

For example, on your £2410 credit card debt making a minimum payment with a 30% APR will take 101 Months (8 Years and 5 months!!) with £3600 in interest However paying £100 per month would reduce this to approximately 36 Months (3 years)

Now your brain will tell you to give up by the 5$^{th}$ month as it will not appear you are making a dent in your debt. But don't despair your brain needs a reward to motivate itself.

So what we look at doing is paying of our lowest value card as quickly as possible.

We will look at our £660 credit with minimum payments will take 112 months to pay off (9 ½ years) with £874 interest, however if we start paying £100 per month (that is an additional £85.00) the debt will be gone within 9 months and we will have only paid £60.00 in interest, our brain will react positively to this as it can see the amount going down quite quickly.

Once this has been paid off you can move this money you were paying and add it to Card 2 which has the highest APR and pay £200 per month to clear this one down, the payments will mean this card will be cleared within 15 Months. Which means we will only pay £423 in interest against £3600

Then you can put all the money of an additional £200 on to the last card and it will clear down within 11 months, but more importantly you will be in a flexible position with your finances and have some breathing space.

As you can see there is no quick fix, but what we can do is get our brain to see the changes and react positively to the debt.

But how can I overpay when I am barely meeting the minimum payment as it is you ask, well reader this is what we will come onto in our next few chapters.

And please remember to break down the large goal to smaller manageable chunks and celebrate those small wins as you will be motivated even more than before if you do this.

## 6, Reducing Fixed and variable costs

This will always be the toughest as there is not really much you can do here, now some people will say get rid of your phone, broadband, Netflix etc.

However, I am a realist you have to understand it is ok to have these things, but one thing if I had it that I would get rid of is any additional cable/sky tv costs. You can move remove these packages or negotiate a lower cost at the end of your contract. Do not be afraid to walk away from them, after all there is so much content available online for free now and you can always go for the pay as you watch option,

I understand this will be tough for some people. But I challenge you to list the channels you watch on a regular basis and whether you can get that content elsewhere.

For example, I know of one person who goes to a bar and drinks one juice whilst watching the sports game (I realise that is an extreme example!) but how much TV do you actually need to watch, could you watch the highlights later for free?

Your mobile phone is another example where you can save costs. when it is time to upgrade could you get a cheaper deal by taking a sim only deal for 12 months, is having the same phone for an additional 12 months going to hurt you?

Using Price comparison sites is great for your vehicle insurance, mobile phone and gas/electric.

One thing I am a big advocate which will involve spending a small amount of money, especially if you have children is getting life insurance for yourself,

You have to ask yourself if the worst happened do you want your children and/or partner to be struggling along to find either the funeral expenses and be in a worst situation financially than you are now after all remember unsecured debt does not mean it goes away should you die, they will and can have a claim on your estate as a lender.

Seriously it is worth spending the cost of one takeaway a month on peace of mind for your children/partners future.

Reducing Other costs

Ok so we hopefully have managed to save a small amount of money on our fixed costs (Remember it all helps!)

We now move on to our variable costs and the first thing we need to look at is our grocery shop, this will be your biggest expense outside of fixed bills. We are creatures of habit in this department, you go shopping to the same supermarket at approximately the same time each week, right?

Ask yourself how long you have been doing this 12 months, 18 months, 5 years?

Well it is time to break this cycle. Next time you need to go shopping make a meal plan for the week and do a list (Do not divulge from this!) remember you do not need to buy a flashy cookbook there are plenty of websites offering recipes for free!

Then go to a budget supermarket and buy as much as you can off of the list, don't worry about brands (you will be surprised by the quality of most of the products on offer from the non-brands) then go to your usual supermarket for the items you could not get, You will be able to reduce your grocery bills by at least 30%, You can then make it a game to see how you can reduce costs further.

Now if you buy something from the budget supermarket and you don't like it that is ok, you know for next time.

Once you have done this a few times I suggest you take a look at your trolley and the biggest expense in there will be most probably meat, Now I am not saying become a vegetarian, but could you look at reducing your intake of meat and have mainly a plant based diet, not only will these reduce your costs, but test have shown reducing your meat consumption also has health benefits.

The other items I would look at cutting out altogether are sugar and fizzy drinks although they are relatively cheap it will help your physical and mental wellbeing.

Clothing will be another big expense, and there are ways of reducing these costs (At the moment we are having to ignore the ethics and morality behind cheaper clothing as we are currently not in a position to be picky!!)

But please remember sometimes the more expensive item will last longer and therefore work out cheaper but it will be up to you to decide and work this out.

Now this will make you think; do you buy lots of clothes? (Studies have shown we wear 20% of our clothing 80% of the time) How many times have you worn your most expensive item?

Could you sell on some items you no longer wear, this will free up space but also give you some additional cash you could reinvest in new items. Charity and thrift shops no longer have the stigma attached to them and you can get some great clothes in these nowadays.

The other time to look is in January when most shops are heavily discounting there clothing or look at the end of winter for purchasing for the following winter and the same with spring/summer.

Please remember our priority at the moment is removing debt, after all most people won't care if you wear the same outfit, as an experiment just make a mental note of when you see your friends, will they always be wearing a new outfit (I doubt it!)

## 7 Prioritise

Now this is the one you can do quite easily, this is not about prioritising your debt (we have just covered this) This is about the additional spending such as nights out, restaurant, birthdays, holidays, Christmas etc.

Again, other books would have you living like a hermit, this is not one of them, remember what I said at the beginning most people spend an additional 10% of net salary a month, well this is the first thing we need to look at reducing,

Holidays and days/nights out

I am not saying do not do these (you have to stay sane somehow!) but could you change your expectations, for example instead of trying to get out to a beach holiday (Let's be honest with ourselves this probably helped put you in this position in the first place) Could you either stay at home and do days out or explore somewhere you have never been before in your own country.

After all, if you ask your children or partner all they care about is spending time with you!

I mean is your partner with you for all the holidays you go on (If they are, I suggest a relationship check!) or are they with you because of you!

I will give you an example a typical holiday in August to go abroad for a family of four from the UK. This will set you back at a minimum £800 per person so for the four people, so a week in the sun will be £3200 excluding spending money so around £3700 to £4000 in total,

Take an extreme example of a holiday in Cornwall or a popular tourist area in the UK in the same period would be £2000 for a cottage plus spending money so £2500 to £3000 in total,

However, if you look at somewhere different within the UK or indeed mainland Europe a rental cottage would be around £800 for the same period plus expenses so worst case £1500 in total, saving you £2500 for one week of beach holiday abroad,

Before you look to complain about the weather you would be surprised at how warm it will get in places in the Summer, you have to ask yourself what is your main goal in going away is it to be with your family or have guaranteed sunshine?

My point is you can find some great deals off the beat and track if you look. Distance too far to drive in a day, you could take advantage of booking hotels early (One hotel chain offers £35 a night if you choose the right venue in advance) The internet has made it so easy now in searching for hotels and rentals and comparing prices of each of them.

If someone offered you £2500 to holiday in the UK for a week I wonder if you would turn it down? I expect not and this is the mind set you need to teach yourself.

Days out,

Other books would have you sat at home and do nothing, but as you can see this book is about reality and not economics!!

Now we know days out can be expensive, so how do we reduce this cost, there are several ways, Firstly look at if it is worth paying for a year subscription if it is a place you will go a few times (Generally 3 visits to the same place will get your money back) and if they have other places of interest (I am a member of

the National Trust and the WWT in the UK as both offer us value for money on regular visits, also the NT is great for day trips to different places)

The other option for special days out are using vouchers (think cereal boxes) and club points (Nectar/Tesco etc..) But just remember always take your own food, we will however buy a hot drink and an ice cream when we are there but everything else, we take with us.

The other places to remember are woods and parks, generally they will be free and get you out into the fresh air. If it is raining board games and crafts are good (you can pick up great games at Charity shops for not a lot of money)

Eating out,

This can be a big expense the average meal out now can easily come to £100 for a family of four. So, what can we do, the simple thing is to look at how many times you either eat out, or order takeaways and the cost associated?

Eating out is a luxury and should be treated as one, however we have become quite complacent in this regard, think back to your own childhood did you eat out a lot or was it for special occasions?

Let's say we had 2 takeaways a month and ate out twice a month also the average cost would be £300 for this a month, If we reduce this to eating out once a month and one takeaway a month we have halved this to £150 but this is still quite high.

There are ways we can reduce it further, look for restaurants that offer early bird deals or 2 for 1 on meals. Look for apps and websites that will offer 2 for 1 on restaurants at certain times.

If you are fond of takeaways look at buying them from your supermarket you will save at least 50% on the mark up and they will taste very similar in most cases. Doing these few things will reduce your spending to £70.00 a month on your eating out/takeaway

If someone said they would pay you £230 per month on you only eating out once and having a supermarket takeaway what would you say?

Birthdays and Christmas

Depending on the age of your children this is a tester for any parent. You want to buy them something extra special but guess what, they don't care!! You do not have to feel guilty for buying something second hand for birthday or Christmas. If it does not come in the original box, print a picture and tape it to the box, but really all they want to see is what is in the packaging. Remember these times are about family being together.

Christmas will generally be the hardest time of all. So how do you deal with it, firstly let me say you are not alone, the pressure from commercial enterprises is very high, so take a deep breath, decide how many presents you want to buy (Think back to the previous year, how many did they play with that you bought, not all of them I bet)

I think 4- 5 presents would be enough, I would suggest maybe one or two new ones. Mixed with a couple of second-hand gifts or handmade ones. Also, do not wait until December to start buying, we generally will start in September when the deals are on. You will be surprised at the deals around for September as the schools are back and it is in general one of the quietest times for shops. Pricing will often be lower than Black Friday deals.

Imagine it comes to December and you have pretty much bought everything, no extra pressure on your accounts with spending. How good would that be, it just requires discipline

Coffee Chains and drinking out.

Addicted to Starbucks, Costa, Nero etc.? How many times do you use them? Once a month, twice a month, Once a week, twice a week? How much do you spend?

Let's say you buy from a chain twice a week at an average of £3.50 each time, not a lot, right

This is you spending £180 a year on a hot beverage? Could you do reduce it to once a week? That's an extra £90 in to your account.

And the Final one the Gym Membership this one it is time to use it or lose it! I am not one to advocate cancelling something if it is being used regularly but if you are paying £30.00 per month and going once a week would you be better of with a pay as you go type system or finding a local park with free weight machines. Also do not cancel because you feel the pressure as we know that exercise is good for the brin and can help keep us in a positive frame of mind.

## 8, Be realistic

As you can see above, we are not saying do not have a life but we need to ensure they we will be realistic with our goals. Remember our brain, the fantastic item we have in our head. It is also our worst enemy you have to remember that our emotional side of our brain is stronger than our rational side, this is down to evolution, yes, our emotional side of our brain developed over thousands of years,

Most purchases are made emotionally and not rationally, watch an advert and you will see it is targeting the emotions and showing you a picture of a successful life, it is telling you to buy this item and you will be happy. Not buy this because it makes sense financially.

When have you seen an advert with the man hunched over the desk looking at a spreadsheet seeing if the next car purchase is worth doing, no it is generally an open road with smiling people with no care in the world?

We need to understand that the purchases are made by our strong side of the brain, remember when you felt guilty after buying something that is your rational side trying to kick in but it is generally too late, and then you tell yourself it won't hurt anyone, or next time I will be stronger and the feeling goes away? Blame the emotional side.

So how do we stop this happening. Well quite simply we need to be aware of it by being self-aware when looking to buy something.

Buying from eBay late at night when you are tired or been drinking, remove the app from your phone, take away the temptation?

Example

Below are some questions you could ask yourself before buying that impulse purchase in a shop that looks like a great deal.

Stop and ask yourself do I really need this at this moment in my life?

Could I afford two of them?

Would this money be better spent elsewhere?

Do I feel positive about the purchase?

If the answer is yes then researching the item and check the reviews, see if you could buy second hand and then look at other retailer prices for the same product to see if it is cheaper elsewhere.

The other thing to do is wait 24 hours and then revisit the item in question.

## 9, Set Goals

Now we have understood where we are financially how much debt we have and our outgoings and we have been able to reduce costs, the time has come to set some goals. Why do we need goals well quite simply it keeps us motivated and hungry to succeed?

I would sit down and working out what your goal for 3 months, 6 months, 9 months and twelve months will be financially,

It can be as simple as we will reduce our takeaways to once a week for 3 months to see what happens, and before you know it is a habit.

One I would like you to try is to save at the same time as you are clearing your debt down. Now again other books will claim that you should clear down all your debt first and then look at saving. However, these books do not take into account your emotional side.

What I suggest you do is when you are in the bank opening up your joint account and asking about the APR on your credit card, ask to open a joint savings account?

With this account I would like you to transfer in month 1, 1% of your joint income, so for example with the £2450 in earnings transfer £24.50 to the savings account and try not to touch it, month 2 try and transfer 2% in to the account, month 3 try 3%. By month 12 you would be putting away almost £300 and should have a savings pot of approximately £1900.

Now don't worry if you miss a month, don't try and catch up just start again at 1% but this is what banks call compounding so you are not just putting in 1% each month you are trying to stretch it, If you do get to the £1900 fantastic treat yourself to a meal (though by this time you will be the master at eating out on a budget so look forward to seeing you using one of the apps that offer discounts!)

Also try this saving trick with your loved ones or children to show them how compounding works) on day one save 1p, 2p on your second day, 3p on your third day, day 100 would be £1.00 Etc... by day 365 you will be at £3.65 now you will have £667.95 saved up by compounding (more on compounding in chapter 11 ) if two of you try this that will be £1335.90 just from starting with a penny. (I will put a chart at the back of the book for use)

If you can carry on the 10% saving each month you will have gone from overspending by 10% a month to saving 10% a month (Effectively you have reduced outgoings by 20% and have you reduced your living standard? probably a bit, but are you happier?)

Now what do you do with this money if you have followed this plan you would have paid off one card already and have a balance outstanding of £1500 on the other with around £2300 still owing on the largest,

My suggestion would be to pay of a balance of one off the cards but ensure it will still leave you with some savings. So, in the space of 12 months you have paid off 2 credit cards with one left!?

## 10 Understanding APR

APR (Annual Percentage Rate) can be confusing for someone who is not in finance, put simply this is the percentage the company charges you for the credit card or loan to be paid back on top of the amount borrowed.

Credit Cards and loans differ in this in the fact that a loan is fixed term borrowing (You decide how much to pay back and when the loan finishes)

Credit Cards are what I class as a flexible loan as you can use them for cash, purchases or balance transfers   All will have different APR's attached to them, you can pay back quickly with no charge or pay in instalments to suit you as long as you pay the minimum payment (banks prefer this as they make more money from you as we saw in chapter 3)

Example

Credit cards will state there APR but what they do is break it down per month so if it is advertised at 20% APR this means on any purchases that are not cleared down on the statement you will be shown an APR of 1.67%, However all credit card companies actually break it down by day as they divide by 365 (days in the year), but the amount total may look similar to your monthly APR they are actually making more money from you due to the compounding effect.

Example

John purchases £500.00 of computer equipment but elects to only clear down £200.00 of this on the statement when it is due, this means that on his next statement he will have been charged for the borrowing of £300.00 at 1.67% which should be £5.15, except as it is a daily rate with compounding it is actually £5.67

So how does this work. (More on this in chapter 12)

On day one John would owe £300.16p on day two the credit card company would take the £300.16p and add the interest to that so it would be now £300.33p and so on.

## 11, Income Streams

Now we can look at income streams, what do I mean by this, well this is your opportunity to look at additional revenues you can bring into your household to ease the financial burden but help long term with your planning,

The goal is to have income coming in that eventually will match not only your monthly outgoings but over time exceed your total income meaning you do not have to rely on your job as your main income stream.

Imagine if in 12 months' time you could walk into your boss and quit your job to follow a passion.

So how do we draw in additional revenue?

There are several ways (By the way none of these will be easy and will require commitment) but let me ask you would you rather sit in front of the television each night worrying about your finances or spend 3 nights in an evening working on an idea? (We spend an average 4 hours a day watching TV, that is around 13 years of your life!!)

You need to ask yourself what are you good at? Please remember we are all good at something. Is it baking, is it reading can you spot mistakes easily (If you can I would be grateful if you could email me with the ones in this book!)

Are you good at organising?

The beauty of the internet it has opened up so many possibilities for people to get additional revenues, whether it be bidding for work on Fiverr or Freelancer (Other sites are available) or indeed using these services to help your idea get off the ground?

The other way to get additional income streams is to write a book (It has never been easier to self-publish)

Do you write about what you know or an interest you have there is plenty of free advice about this, one person whom followed the above published a book on inspirational quotes he collected from famous people using the internet to research and this became a best seller which meant he could by his home outright and work part time.

But whatever you do commit to it and don't get disheartened if it doesn't work out, hey you could always write a book about your journey!

Whatever you choose to do be positive about it and remember you have probably done something few people in their lifetime will try and you will have learned from it, also remember success does not come to you overnight, you only have to look at big YouTube stars and go to their first videos they shot to see how rough they were and how few views they had, success takes time but with focus and determination your hobby will help you unwind and open you up to more creative ideas.

The other one is buying and selling online.

Example

I know of someone who used Alibaba and bought some owl necklaces (100) at £.30p each including postage, so £30.00 all in, they then advertised them on eBay at £1.50 excluding postage and packing,

When they sold all of them, they had made a profit of £120.00 now this does not sound like a lot but that means they now have £120.00 to invest in other products online to sell.

Most people do not go down the route of starting their own business because they make excuses, but when you question them, they admit it is the fact they have not started as the feel embarrassment if friends and family find out because they feel that the business is to small, what you have to understand is we have to start somewhere.

If I said to you by the end of tomorrow, I will give you a million pounds if you could tell me three things you are good at that could make money, I am sure you would come up with them!

So, what are you waiting for!!

## 12 Savings, Pensions and compounding

Hopefully you are now in a position after hard work and a small amount of sacrifice where we have some regular savings coming in.

I would then look to the future and your retirement, after all we have to be realistic and realise the government are not going to help us be in a position where we can live the lifestyle we are used to.

Nor do we want to find ourselves in a position we have been in previously with debt hanging over our shoulders

I suggest that you look at putting around 20% off your savings into a pension plan, I would suggest you seek an independent financial advisor for this, one who is FCA approved and I would ask if he is rewarded by any scheme he recommends?

Or you can go on the internet and find your own pension plan to use, some countries now have companies using auto enrol to get you into some type of pension scheme and it will always be worth investing in that one first directly from your salary.

Then we will look at diversifying our other savings into investments (such as property or high interest accounts) at a percentage you feel comfortable with. Remember to keep some savings back though for when times are hard, after all we do not want all our hard work to go to waste now.

If you are not sure it is worth seeking out professional advice in this area.

Compounding

Albert Einstein once called compounding the eighth wonder of the world and said "He who understands it earns it, he who doesn't pays it"

To make compounding work for you, you need to keep adding money, but by doing this your money works for you.

Example

If you invest £1000 on a 7% annual return, by year 5 you would have your interest risen from £70 to £92 a year an increase of 31%.

If you look at the penny a day compound this is the best way to understand the power of compounding. (as shown in chapter 9) Also there is a spreadsheet at the back of this book to show you.

The other good exercise to show the power of compounding is the 1p doubled every day and below I have put this one show you the power of compounding

Day 1     1p

Day 2     2p

Day 3     4p

Day 4     8p

Day 5     16p

By day 10 it is up to £10.24 by Day 20 you would be up to £5,242.88 by Day 30 the pot would be at £5,368,709

That is over £5 million pounds in 30 days just from starting with 1p, now we are not in a position to put that amount of money in yet, but it gives you an idea of the power of compounding your money.

It also shows you the power that banks have when they compound interest (This is why on a mortgage even though the rate may be 4-5% you will actually pay almost double what you borrowed)

## 13, Using Apps to help

There are plenty of apps that can help you on your journey, I have listed a few below to consider (Please note these are all free, I do not fell write proposing paid for apps especially when we are trying to save money, Also I am not affiliated with any of the below, nor am I being paid to recommend them)

Mint (US and Canada only) This allows you to do a budget and connect all your bank accounts to one place

Curve App (EU Only) a great App that lets you put all your cards on one device and you can see the spend daily, weekly and monthly

Wally (Available Worldwide) Wally is personal finance app that helps you keep track of your finances

Acorns (US and Australia) Acorns allows you ot round up spending and invest the spare change in the stock market.

Moneyboxapp (UK only) Moneybox app is very similar to Acorns but for the UK only.

Now I know there will be others out there and feel free to drop me an email if you find one that works for you,

Remember everyone is different but the important thing to keep in mind is the ability to record and check your spending.

## 14, How to remain debt free (Money can't buy you happiness but!)

By now you have put in place the processes I have talked about and it is 18 months later, you are in a healthy position financially, your debt is near enough non-existent. How do you keep it that way?

Well the good news is you have done the hardest part you have believed in yourself and what you can do and achieve, remember it is a mindset.

Example

If you look at most self-made millionaires, they have been declared bankrupt or lost most of there wealth at one stage or another, the thing that made them carry on is that they backed themselves with their own belief.

You need to believe in yourself and see money as an asset to be held on to rather than having an attitude of it will be alright!

Example

Bernie Ecclestone a multi billionaire once owned Queens Park Rangers that at the time were playing football in the English premier league. He arrived at the stadium on and was shown around, in the players dressing room he noticed bottles of water, Who pays for that he asked, We do came the reply, how much does that cost us, £0.65p each was the answer, Bernie then asked what was wrong with tap water!, he also found out that they paid for the wives and girlfriends to have lunch at £3.65per head, he also put a stop to this, this was costing the club less then £5000.00 per year.

Warren Buffet who is worth close to 90 billion dollars flies economy unless someone else is paying, he will even collect people from the airport himself sometimes.

The above are examples where people hold on to there money yet will spend other peoples, now these are two extreme examples but I wanted to show you the sort of mindset that you need to be extremely wealthy.

Please note although they may look tight, they do in fact donate large amounts of money to charity each year as well, but they know when something is of value and something is not.

You have heard the phrase Money can't buy you happiness, right?

Well it is partly true, it cannot buy you happiness but it can buy you three things that you will struggle to get without it!

Time,

Having money means you can use your time more wisely to create more wealth or spend more time with your family, by this I mean you can hire people to do chores, such as cleaning, ironing gardening etc... this then will free you up to concentrate on your financial goals

Freedom

Being Financially sound means you have freedom and choice to choose what you want to do and where you want to go, you will often hear people say that they are financially free, this can mean different things to different people,

Choice

You have the choice to work or not work due to the stability of your finances, it will open doors to opportunities you can choose to pursue with new contacts you can choose to talk to or listen to. It will open up doors to further choices whether it be working with someone on a new project or idea, to having someone run your company for you?

**15, Spread sheets can help**

You can use spreadsheets to help track your spending or apps or even a notebook and pen, but one thing I will say is you will need to track your spending, that way you will be able to identify where you are spending frivolously against where the spend is needed. After a couple of months, you will be a master at this and gleefully telling people where the cheapest buys are!!

# 16 Reference Material

Debt Help

There are many companies out there who will offer to help, always try and go with one that is on your Government website as these in the whole will either be free or not for profit.

Do not be afraid to ask if there is a cost especially with companies that are pushing you for a consolidation plan or involuntary agreement as that is how they will be making their money.

Listed below are some details for different countries on debt advice.

United States

You will be able to find free or low-cost advice at Credit Unions or non-profit agencies, just ensure that they are accredited to either the

National foundation for credit counselling (NFCC) https://www.nfcc.org/

or the Financial Counselling association of America (FCAA)     https://fcaa.org/

Canada

I would recommend using a not for profit organisation, Credit Counselling Canada is the national association of not for profit in Canada and are regulated by the Government of Canada

https://creditcounsellingcanada.ca/

#

Australia

The National Debt Helpline is your best contact this is run by the Australian government, http://www.ndh.org.au/

Free financial counselling is offered throughout Australia via the ASIC (Australia Securities and investment Commission)

https://www.moneysmart.gov.au/managing-your-money/managing-debts/financial-counselling#find

United Kingdom

Step change are a debt advice charity offering free advice
https://www.stepchange.org/

National debt line is another free advice charity
https://www.nationaldebtline.org/

Citizens advice will be able to also offer guidance
https://www.citizensadvice.org.uk/

I am sorry if I have not entered your country and you need help the best place to look for advice will be on your country's main government website.

I hope this book has helped you see light at the end of the tunnel and remember this will not be a quick fix bit with time and perseverance I know you have it in you to be living the life you want!

## 17 Reminders

Have a plan and set goals

Be Positive it is in your power to change your circumstances

Remember to celebrate the small wins

Remember to compound your money!

Focus each day on why you are doing this and what the end goal would mean to you.

Above all enjoy yourself and the challenge that you have set, as you will look back in 6 months and realise how far you have come!

## 18. Materials

| Income | Amount (Fixed) | Total |
|---|---|---|
|  |  |  |
| Salary 1 |  |  |
| Salary 2 |  |  |
| Misc |  |  |
|  |  |  |
| **Total Income** |  |  |
|  |  |  |
| **Fixed Costs** |  |  |
| Mortgage/Rent |  |  |
| Water |  |  |
| Gas/Electricity |  |  |
| Tax |  |  |
| Phone Line |  |  |
| Mobile Phone |  |  |
| Loan |  |  |
| Life Insurance |  |  |
| Medical Insurance |  |  |
| Loan 1 |  |  |
| Loan 2 |  |  |
| Netflix |  |  |
|  |  |  |
| **Sub Total** |  |  |
| **Others** |  |  |
| Food |  |  |
| Fuel |  |  |
| Clothes |  |  |
| Eating Out |  |  |
|  |  |  |
| **Sub Total** |  |  |
|  |  |  |
| **Credit Cards** |  |  |
| CC1 |  |  |
| CC2 |  |  |
| CC3 |  |  |
| **Sub Total** |  |  |
| **Total** |  |  |
| **Total Fixed Costs** |  |  |
| Total Others |  |  |
| Sub Total |  |  |
| Credit Cards Total |  |  |
| Total |  |  |

Budget Guide.

## 1p A Day Challenge Compounding (First 90 days)

| Day | Save | Total | Day | Save | Total | Day | Save | Total |
|---|---|---|---|---|---|---|---|---|
| 1 | £ 0.01 | £ 0.01 | 31 | £ 0.31 | £ 4.96 | 61 | £ 0.61 | £ 18.91 |
| 2 | £ 0.02 | £ 0.03 | 32 | £ 0.32 | £ 5.28 | 62 | £ 0.62 | £ 19.53 |
| 3 | £ 0.03 | £ 0.06 | 33 | £ 0.33 | £ 5.61 | 63 | £ 0.63 | £ 20.16 |
| 4 | £ 0.04 | £ 0.10 | 34 | £ 0.34 | £ 5.95 | 64 | £ 0.64 | £ 20.80 |
| 5 | £ 0.05 | £ 0.15 | 35 | £ 0.35 | £ 6.30 | 65 | £ 0.65 | £ 21.45 |
| 6 | £ 0.06 | £ 0.21 | 36 | £ 0.36 | £ 6.66 | 66 | £ 0.66 | £ 22.11 |
| 7 | £ 0.07 | £ 0.28 | 37 | £ 0.37 | £ 7.03 | 67 | £ 0.67 | £ 22.78 |
| 8 | £ 0.08 | £ 0.36 | 38 | £ 0.38 | £ 7.41 | 68 | £ 0.68 | £ 23.46 |
| 9 | £ 0.09 | £ 0.45 | 39 | £ 0.39 | £ 7.80 | 69 | £ 0.69 | £ 24.15 |
| 10 | £ 0.10 | £ 0.55 | 40 | £ 0.40 | £ 8.20 | 70 | £ 0.70 | £ 24.85 |
| 11 | £ 0.11 | £ 0.66 | 41 | £ 0.41 | £ 8.61 | 71 | £ 0.71 | £ 25.56 |
| 12 | £ 0.12 | £ 0.78 | 42 | £ 0.42 | £ 9.03 | 72 | £ 0.72 | £ 26.28 |
| 13 | £ 0.13 | £ 0.91 | 43 | £ 0.43 | £ 9.46 | 73 | £ 0.73 | £ 27.01 |
| 14 | £ 0.14 | £ 1.05 | 44 | £ 0.44 | £ 9.90 | 74 | £ 0.74 | £ 27.75 |
| 15 | £ 0.15 | £ 1.20 | 45 | £ 0.45 | £ 10.35 | 75 | £ 0.75 | £ 28.50 |
| 16 | £ 0.16 | £ 1.36 | 46 | £ 0.46 | £ 10.81 | 76 | £ 0.76 | £ 29.26 |
| 17 | £ 0.17 | £ 1.53 | 47 | £ 0.47 | £ 11.28 | 77 | £ 0.77 | £ 30.03 |
| 18 | £ 0.18 | £ 1.71 | 48 | £ 0.48 | £ 11.76 | 78 | £ 0.78 | £ 30.81 |
| 19 | £ 0.19 | £ 1.90 | 49 | £ 0.49 | £ 12.25 | 79 | £ 0.79 | £ 31.60 |
| 20 | £ 0.20 | £ 2.10 | 50 | £ 0.50 | £ 12.75 | 80 | £ 0.80 | £ 32.40 |
| 21 | £ 0.21 | £ 2.31 | 51 | £ 0.51 | £ 13.26 | 81 | £ 0.81 | £ 33.21 |
| 22 | £ 0.22 | £ 2.53 | 52 | £ 0.52 | £ 13.78 | 82 | £ 0.82 | £ 34.03 |
| 23 | £ 0.23 | £ 2.76 | 53 | £ 0.53 | £ 14.31 | 83 | £ 0.83 | £ 34.86 |
| 24 | £ 0.24 | £ 3.00 | 54 | £ 0.54 | £ 14.85 | 84 | £ 0.84 | £ 35.70 |
| 25 | £ 0.25 | £ 3.25 | 55 | £ 0.55 | £ 15.40 | 85 | £ 0.85 | £ 36.55 |
| 26 | £ 0.26 | £ 3.51 | 56 | £ 0.56 | £ 15.96 | 86 | £ 0.86 | £ 37.41 |
| 27 | £ 0.27 | £ 3.78 | 57 | £ 0.57 | £ 16.53 | 87 | £ 0.87 | £ 38.28 |
| 28 | £ 0.28 | £ 4.06 | 58 | £ 0.58 | £ 17.11 | 88 | £ 0.88 | £ 39.16 |
| 29 | £ 0.29 | £ 4.35 | 59 | £ 0.59 | £ 17.70 | 89 | £ 0.89 | £ 40.05 |
| 30 | £ 0.30 | £ 4.65 | 60 | £ 0.60 | £ 18.30 | 90 | £ 0.90 | £ 40.95 |

# 1P Double a day for 30 days challenge

| Day | Amount | Total | Day | Amount | Total | Day | Amount | Total |
|---|---|---|---|---|---|---|---|---|
| 1 | £ 0.01 | £ 0.01 | 11 | £ 5.12 | £ 10.24 | 21 | £ 5,242.88 | £ 10,485.76 |
| 2 | £ 0.02 | £ 0.02 | 12 | £ 10.24 | £ 20.48 | 22 | £ 10,485.76 | £ 20,971.52 |
| 3 | £ 0.04 | £ 0.04 | 13 | £ 20.48 | £ 40.96 | 23 | £ 20,971.52 | £ 41,943.04 |
| 4 | £ 0.40 | £ 0.08 | 14 | £ 40.96 | £ 81.92 | 24 | £ 41,943.04 | £ 83,886.08 |
| 5 | £ 0.80 | £ 0.16 | 15 | £ 81.92 | £ 163.84 | 25 | £ 83,886.08 | £ 167,772.16 |
| 6 | £ 0.16 | £ 0.32 | 16 | £ 163.84 | £ 327.68 | 26 | £ 167,772.16 | £ 335,544.32 |
| 7 | £ 0.32 | £ 0.64 | 17 | £ 327.68 | £ 655.36 | 27 | £ 335,544.32 | £ 671,088.64 |
| 8 | £ 0.64 | £ 1.28 | 18 | £ 655.36 | £ 1,310.72 | 28 | £ 671,088.64 | £ 1,342,177.28 |
| 9 | £ 1.28 | £ 2.56 | 19 | £ 1,310.72 | £ 2,621.44 | 29 | £ 1,342,177.28 | £ 2,684,354.56 |
| 10 | £ 2.56 | £ 5.12 | 20 | £ 2,621.44 | £ 5,242.88 | 30 | £ 2,684,354.56 | £ 5,368,709.12 |

www.ingramcontent.com/pod-product-compliance
Lightning Source LLC
Chambersburg PA
CBHW071150220526
45468CB00003B/1014